TRADITION

TRADITION

Orthodox Jewish Life in America / Mal Warshaw

SCHOCKEN BOOKS / NEW YORK

First published by SCHOCKEN BOOKS 1976

Library of Congress Cataloging in Publication Data

Warshaw, Mal.
Tradition: Orthodox Jewish life in America.

1. Orthodox Judaism—United States—Pictorial works.
2. Jews in Brooklyn—Pictorial works. 3. Jews—Rites
and ceremonies—Pictorial works. 4. United States—
Religious life and customs—Pictorial works. 5.
Brooklyn—Description—Views. I. Title.

BM205.W26 974.7 '23 '004924 76-9130

Published in association with the exhibition

Tradition: Photographs by Mal Warshaw of the Lubavitch in Brooklyn

The Brooklyn Museum, September 24–November 28, 1976

Printed in the United States of America

To my wife, Betty

Preface

Accident or fate in the guise of a friend on an errand brought me to Crown Heights, in Brooklyn, three years ago. Although I am a native New Yorker and I have lived in this city all my life, this neighborhood was totally new to me and worlds away from the New York I knew. It was for me instantly exciting. I was fascinated by the immediate and cliché observation—the way in which my visual perceptions were suddenly and vividly eighteenth-century European and at the same time so obviously urban twentieth-century New York. The shifting time frames were literally eye-blinks away.

I returned with my camera again and again. I made close friends among the devout Jews I met, was invited to participate in their family and community celebrations, and was made to feel at home with the routines of daily life in this other New York. What had begun as a flirtation with the exotic became a transforming experience. Although their modes could never be mine, the quality of my life has been enhanced by the warmth of their friendship, the lessons they taught me so patiently, and their uncritical acceptance of such an untutored Jew.

Nowhere else had I witnessed such an intimacy with God and seen such joy in the most ordinary daily routines. I was awed by the strength of their commitment to God and tradition and amazed by such single-purposed adherence to so simple a way of life—a way of life which had stubbornly and devotedly resisted the threats of annihilation in the Holocaust, the temptations of assimilation in America, and the ongoing lures of modernity.

The intensity of Jewish experience in that community and other similar communities, it seems to me, must be the wellspring for the various and diluted forms of Jewish orthodox experience I suddenly newly discovered all over the city. The photographs shown here are the result of a two-year exploration. I have tried to record faithfully the ingredients of the mystery. For if there is a secret to the Jewish genius for survival, I suspect the answer can be found there.

Most of the photographs for this book were taken candidly in the ordinary course of daily life or during the performance of religious rituals and obligations; however, in a few cases, when religious law would have forbidden photographing, such as the holy days of Rosh Hashanah and Yom Kippur, I had to be content with photographing around the occasions themselves. In some other instances, such as the Sabbath and Passover, some people were kind enough to enact rituals at other times. I wish to thank all those who permitted me to photograph them both abroad and at home. I am especially grateful to Rabbi Yehuda Krinsky and his family, to Rabbi Shmarya Shusterman and his family, and to Rabbi Sholem Ber Hecht and his family.

MAL WARSHAW

January, 1976

Contents

TRADITION

1
The Torah

These are the testimonies, and the statutes, and the ordinances, which Moses spoke unto the children of Israel, when they came forth out of Egypt.

—DEUTERONOMY 4:45

The Torah is the core of Jewish tradition. It contains the covenant with God as revealed to Moses at Sinai. It is the instrument upon which observant Jews base their lives.

The Torah scroll (*Sefer Torah*) that is used in the synagogue is inscribed on parchment by a *sofer* (scribe) who is an authority on the manner in which sacred documents are to be prepared and written.

Before reading the *Sefer Torah*, it is customary to touch it with the *tallit* (prayer shawl) at the place to be read, and then to kiss the *tallit*. This is done as a sign of love for the Torah.

The institution of reading the *Sefer Torah* in the synagogue is a tradition that dates back two thousand years.

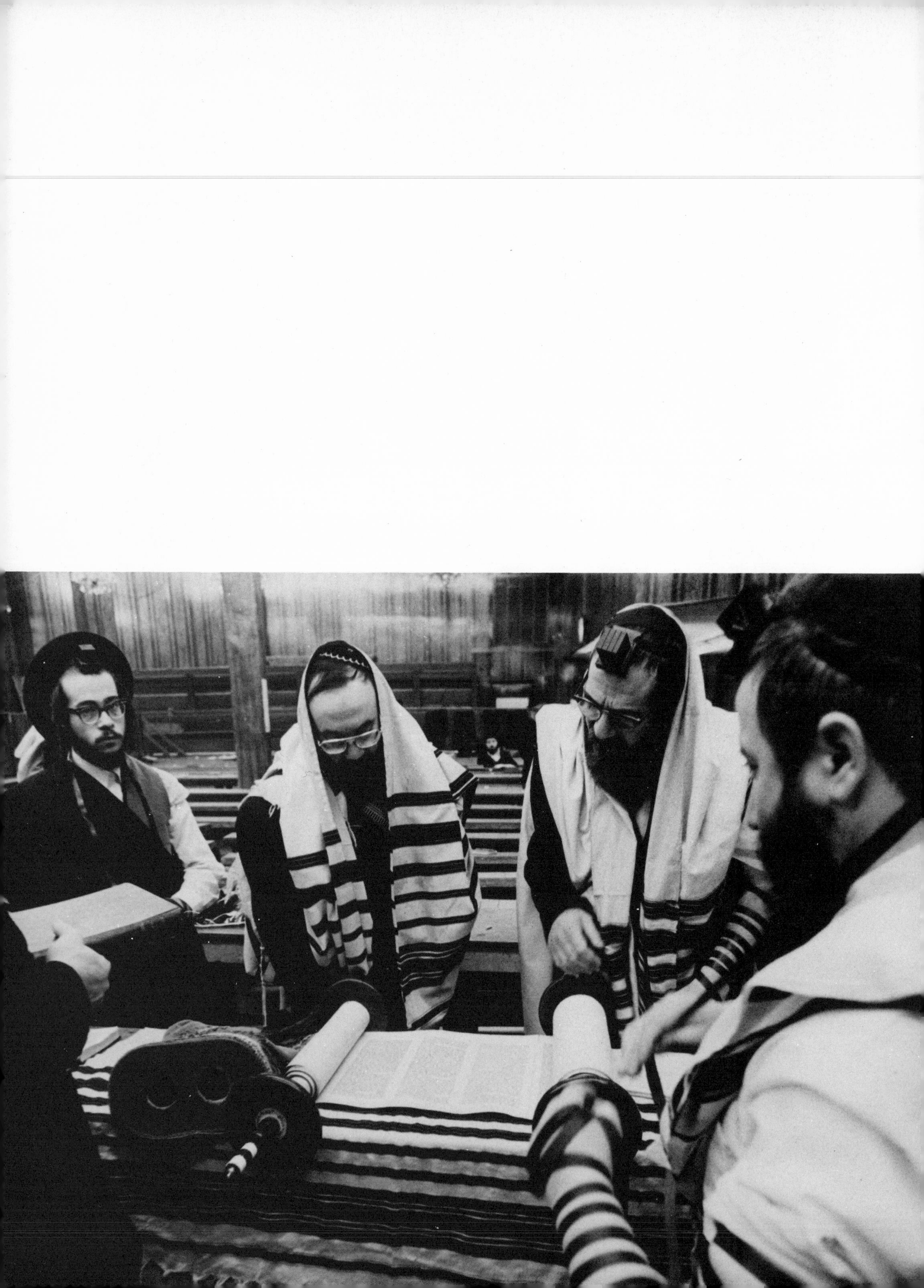

After reading from the Torah, the scroll is raised so that all the worshipers can see the script.

The trappings that contain the *Sefer Torah* are richly decorated and frequently "crowned."

2

Prayer and Study: Synagogue and *Yeshivah*

And let them make me a sanctuary, that I may dwell among them.

—EXODUS 25:8

The synagogue is the center of religious life where Jews meet to pray, meditate, discuss the holy books, and share the ecstasy of an encounter with God.

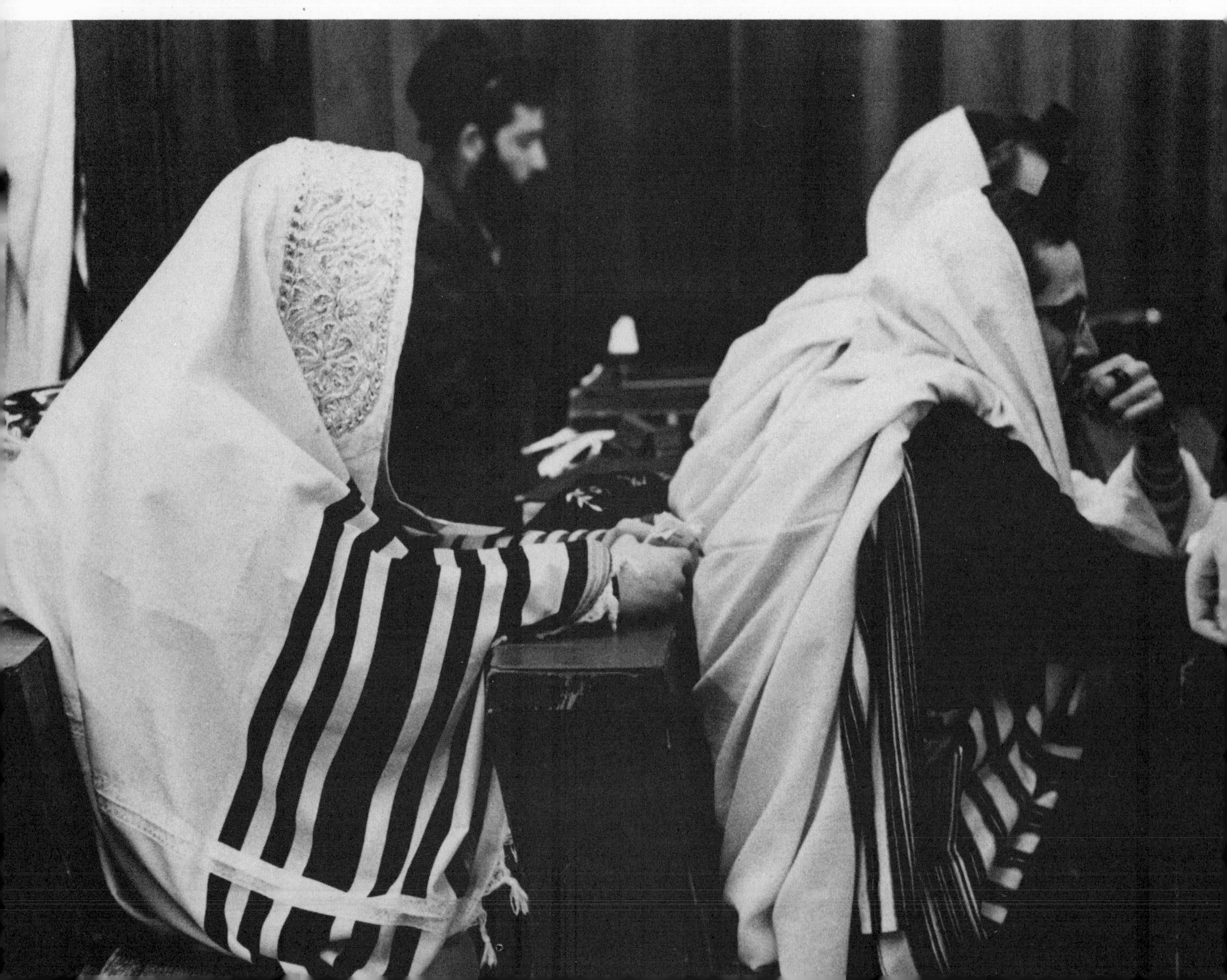

This book of the law shall not depart out of thy mouth, but thou shalt meditate therein day and night, that thou mayest observe to do according to all that is written therein.

—JOSHUA 1:8

The Lubavitch *yeshivah* in Morristown, N.J.

3

Tefillin

And thou shalt bind them for a sign upon thy hand, and they shall be for frontlets between thine eyes.

—DEUTERONOMY 6:8

According to the law, a Jewish boy is required to put on *tefillin* on weekdays from the time he becomes bar mitzvah.

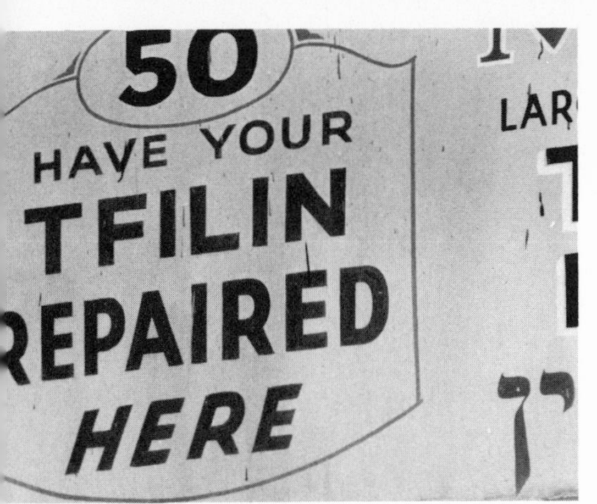

Tefillin consist of two small leather boxes with straps. Each box contains four paragraphs of the Torah inscribed on parchment (Exodus 13:1–10; 13:11–16 and Deuteronomy 6:4–9; 11:13–21).

This is a piece of parchment for *tefillin* on which is inscribed the Jew's duty to remember the redemption from Egyptian bondage.

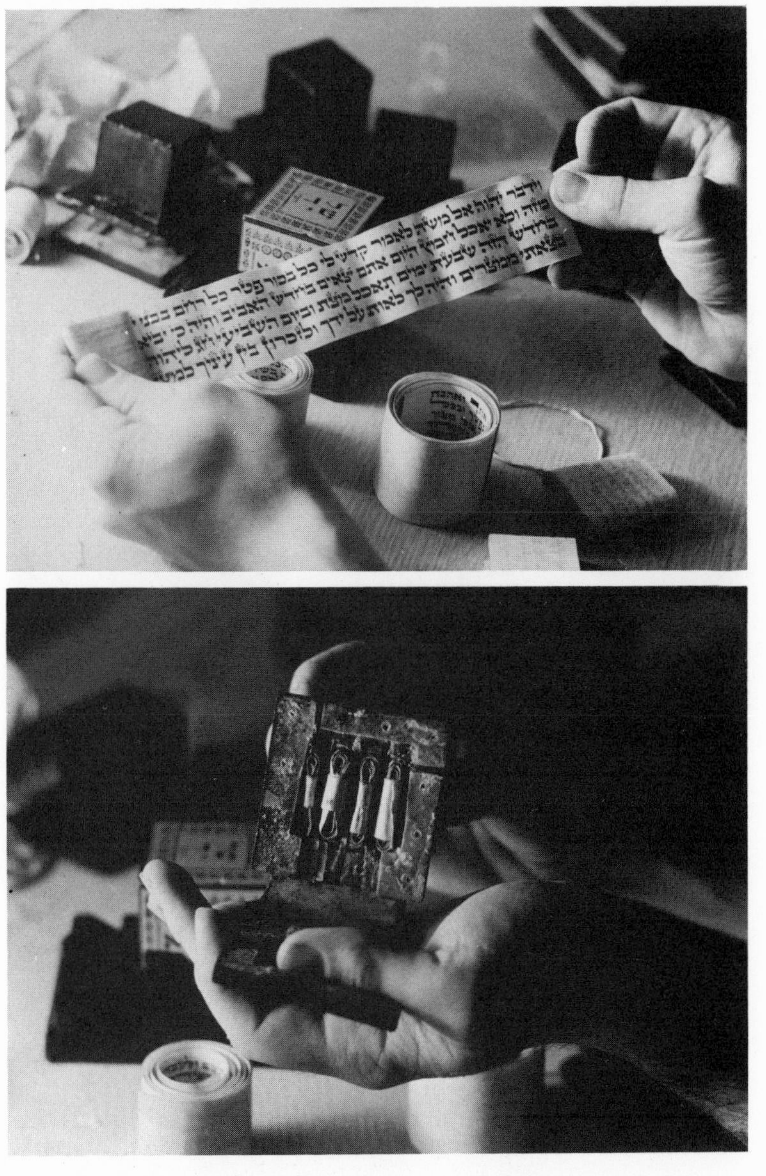

The four pieces of parchment encased in the *tefillin*.

Tefillin are manufactured from the skin of a kosher (fit) animal, and everything associated with the tradition of *tefillin* must also be kosher.

4

Tallit and *Tzitzit*

And the Lord spoke unto Moses, saying: "Speak unto the children of Israel, and bid them that they make them throughout their generations fringes in the corners of their garments, and that they put with the fringe of each corner a thread of blue."
—NUMBERS 15:37–38

Tzitzit, a four-cornered garment with ritual fringes, are worn by orthodox males in accordance with the commandment.

The manner in which *tzitzit* are prepared must conform to traditional law.

The *tallit katan* (or little *tallit*) is worn daily, usually underneath outer clothing.

5

Mezuzah

And thou shalt write them upon the doorposts of thy house, and upon thy gates.

—DEUTERONOMY 6:9

The sanctity of the Jewish home is symbolized by the *mezuzah,* a little scroll affixed to the right doorpost of the entrance and the rooms of a house.

The *mezuzah* is a piece of parchment on which is written two biblical passages (Deuteronomy 6:4–9; 11:13–21).

It is customary, upon entering or leaving the house, to touch the *mezuzah* and kiss one's fingers.

6

Tzedakah

Thou shalt not harden thy heart, nor shut thy hand from thy needy brother.

—DEUTERONOMY 15:7

Tzedakah (charity) is a biblical precept that pervades all aspects of Jewish life.

It is forbidden to turn a poor person away empty-handed.

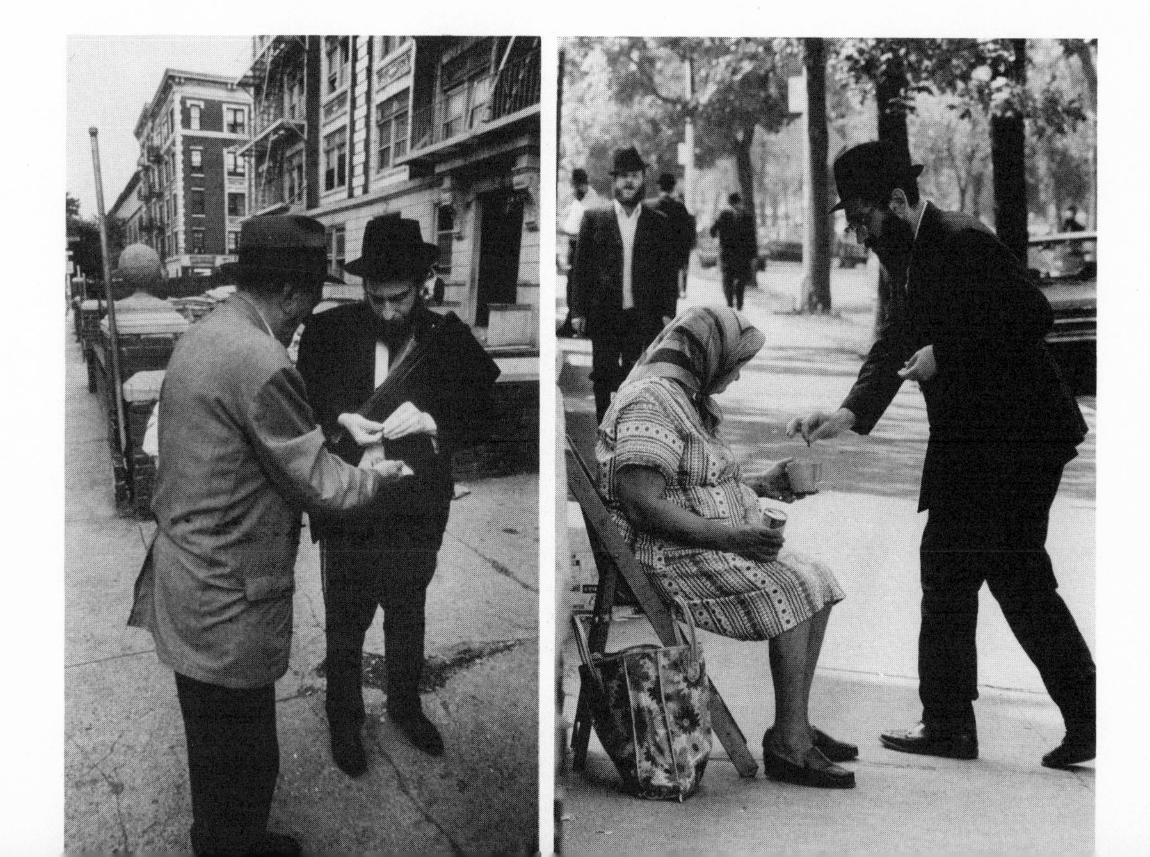

7
Handwashing

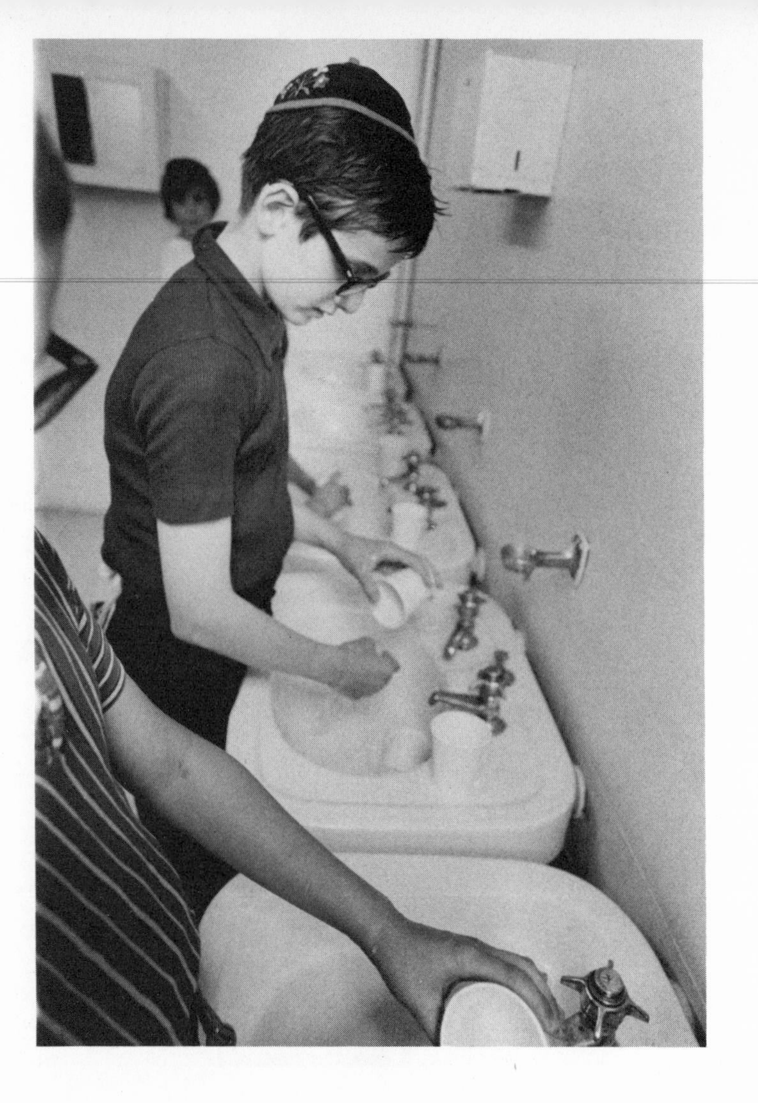

Before eating bread over which the benediction is said, one must wash his hands.

8
Haircut

Ye shall not round the corners of your heads, neither shalt thou mar the corners of thy beard.

—LEVITICUS 19:27

Payes are side locks, grown as prescribed by the Torah.

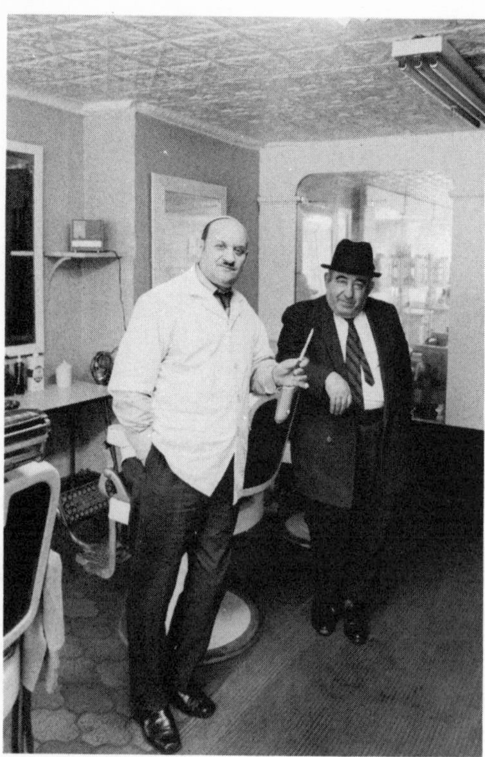

The commandment is the foundation upon which this small barbershop in Brooklyn functions. Its customers vary from Hasidim, for whom removal of the beard would be a breach of faith, to Jews who require conventional grooming.

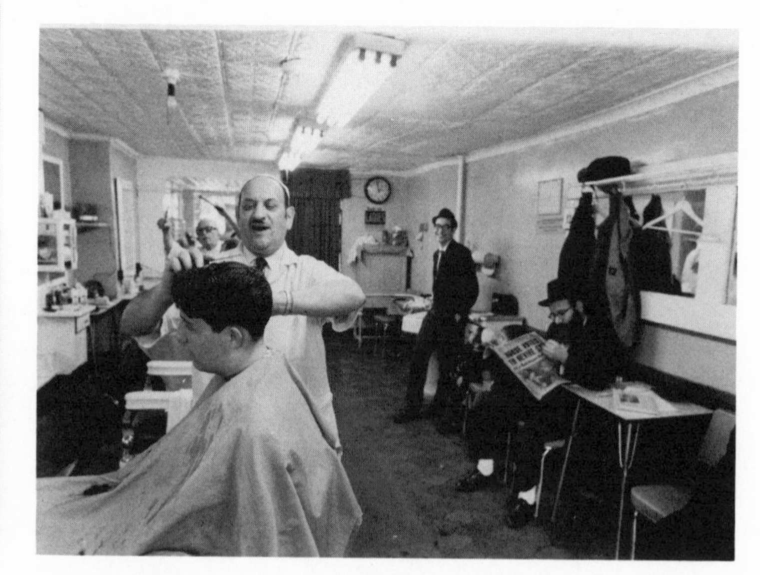

It is a custom to give a boy his first haircut at the age of three. The third birthday is also the time when a boy first wears *tzitzit*.

9

Mikveh

And he shall bathe his flesh in running water, and shall be clean.

—LEVITICUS 15:13

The ritual bath, or *mikveh,* is a small pool of water constructed to the precise requirements of Jewish law and is under the supervision of a competent orthodox authority.

The bathroom is supplied with soap, shampoo, and bleach (for removing stains from the skin) and a plastic block on which to store the *sheitel* (wig) which married Jewish women traditionally wear.

Ritual immersion is regarded as indispensable to religious life. The *mikveh* is used mainly by post-menstruous women and by some orthodox Jews, especially Hasidim, as an aide to purifying the spirit. According to Jewish law, if poverty makes a choice mandatory, it is permitted to sell a synagogue in order to build a mikveh.

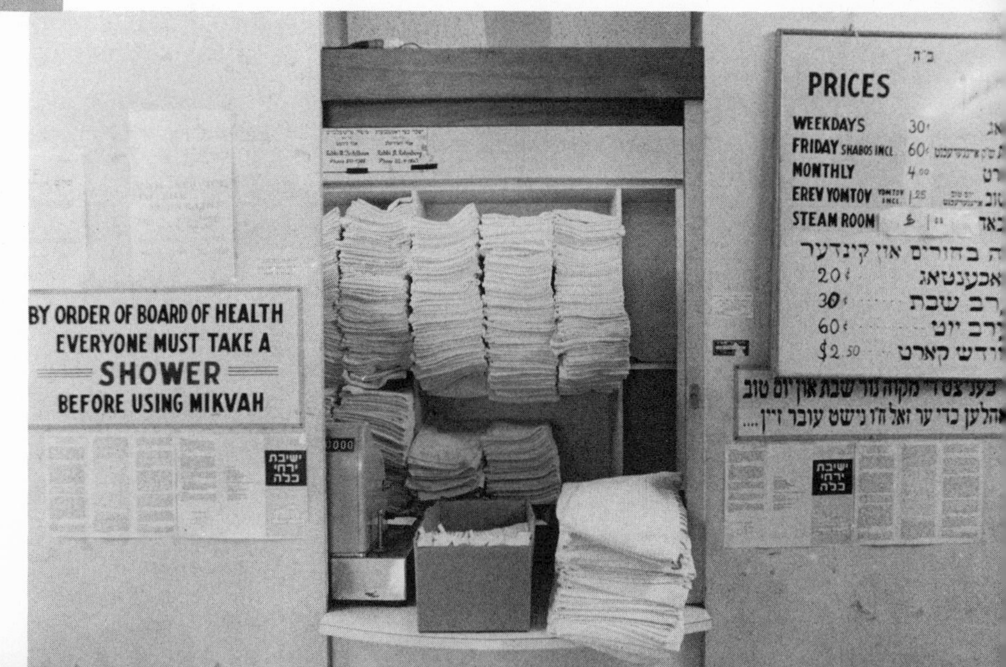

10

Kashrut

To make a difference between the unclean and the clean, and between the living thing that may be eaten and the living thing that may not be eaten.

—LEVITICUS 11:47

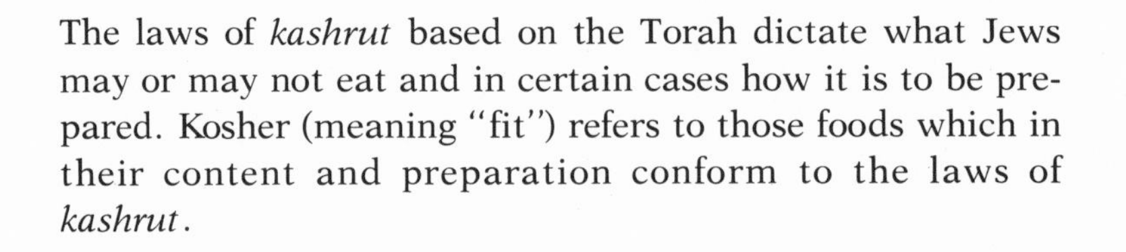

The laws of *kashrut* based on the Torah dictate what Jews may or may not eat and in certain cases how it is to be prepared. Kosher (meaning "fit") refers to those foods which in their content and preparation conform to the laws of *kashrut*.

There are orthodox Jews who are skeptical about the kosher nature of the food available to them. *Glatt kosher* is kosher without a doubt and may be eaten by the most ardent adherent of the dietary laws.

In accordance with the law that forbids the consuming of meat and dairy products at the same meal or from the same utensils, these twin kitchens (one for meat, the other for dairy) were set up in a school in Brooklyn.

11

Shabbos (Sabbath)

Six days shalt thou labor, and do all thy work; but the seventh day is a sabbath unto the Lord thy God.

—EXODUS 20:9–10

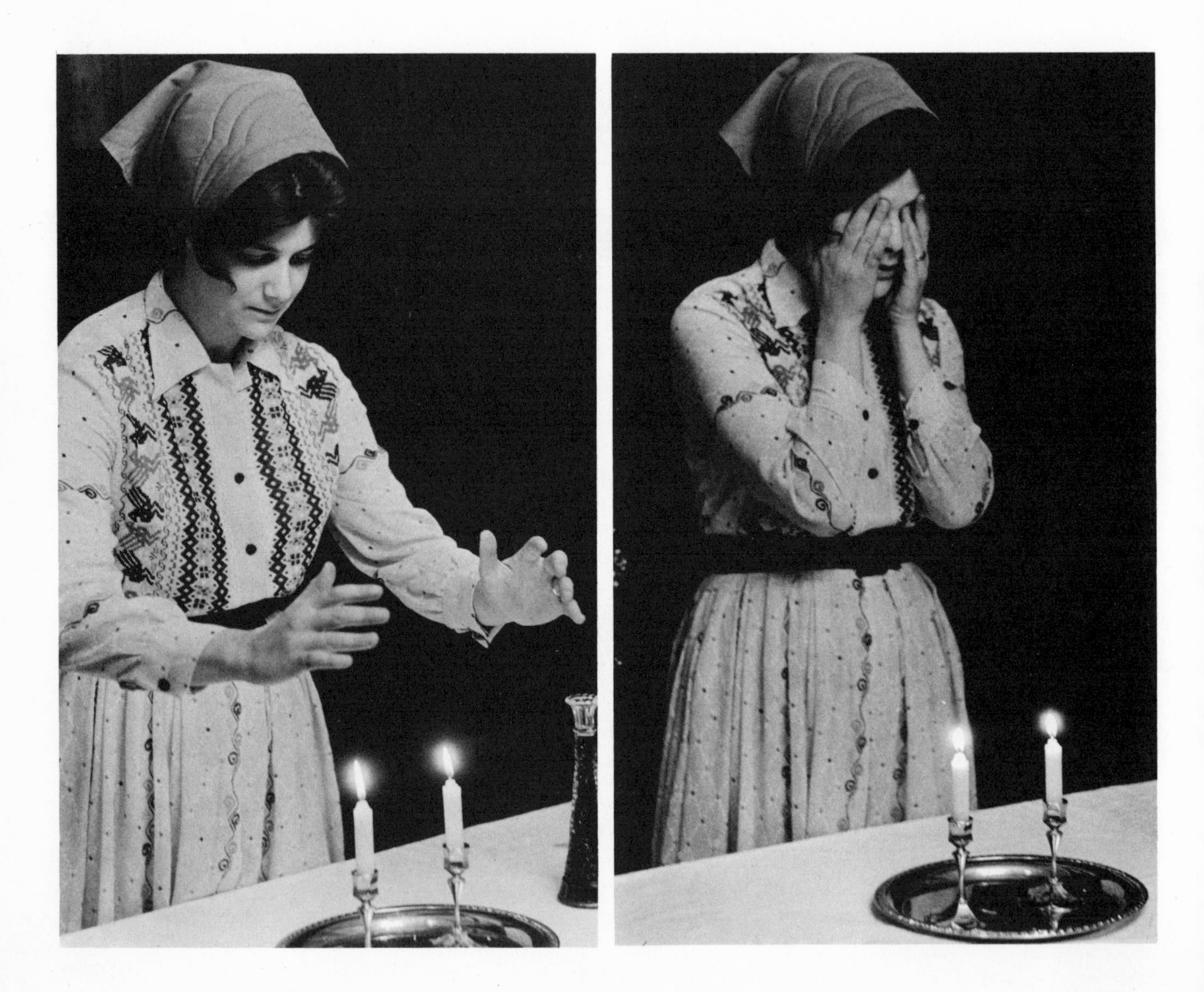

The most familiar religious role of the Jewish wife and mother is lighting the candles, the ritual that formally ushers in the Sabbath.

The Kiddush (Sanctification) is recited over wine.

And the *hallah* is blessed
and dipped in salt before the meal.

Jewish stores are closed in observance of *Shabbos*.

This sign in the Fifth Avenue Synagogue permits the use of the elevator without breaking the commandment that prohibits work.

The Torah forbids a Jew to carry anything on *Shabbos*. How then may a Jew leave his home if he is unable to carry the key away with him?

The solution lies in the making of a tie-clasp, a belt buckle, a woman's pin, designed to fit the lock. It may be worn as an integral part of one's clothing, without violating the Sabbath.

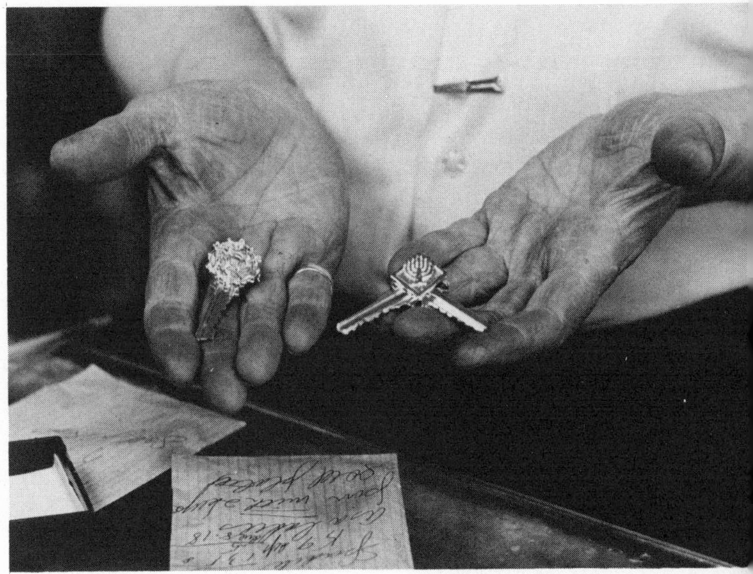

SKI JET
KIDDIE KARNIVAL
SPECIAL
Carousel
GIVE TO YOUR AMERICAN CANCER SOCIETY
Woolite
PARKER PENS
BAYER
SALES
TAX
40
60

Havdalah (which means division, or separation), the ritual that observes the departure of the Sabbath, is performed over a cup of wine and is celebrated with a special candle made of two or more braided wicks, as in this summer camp for girls.

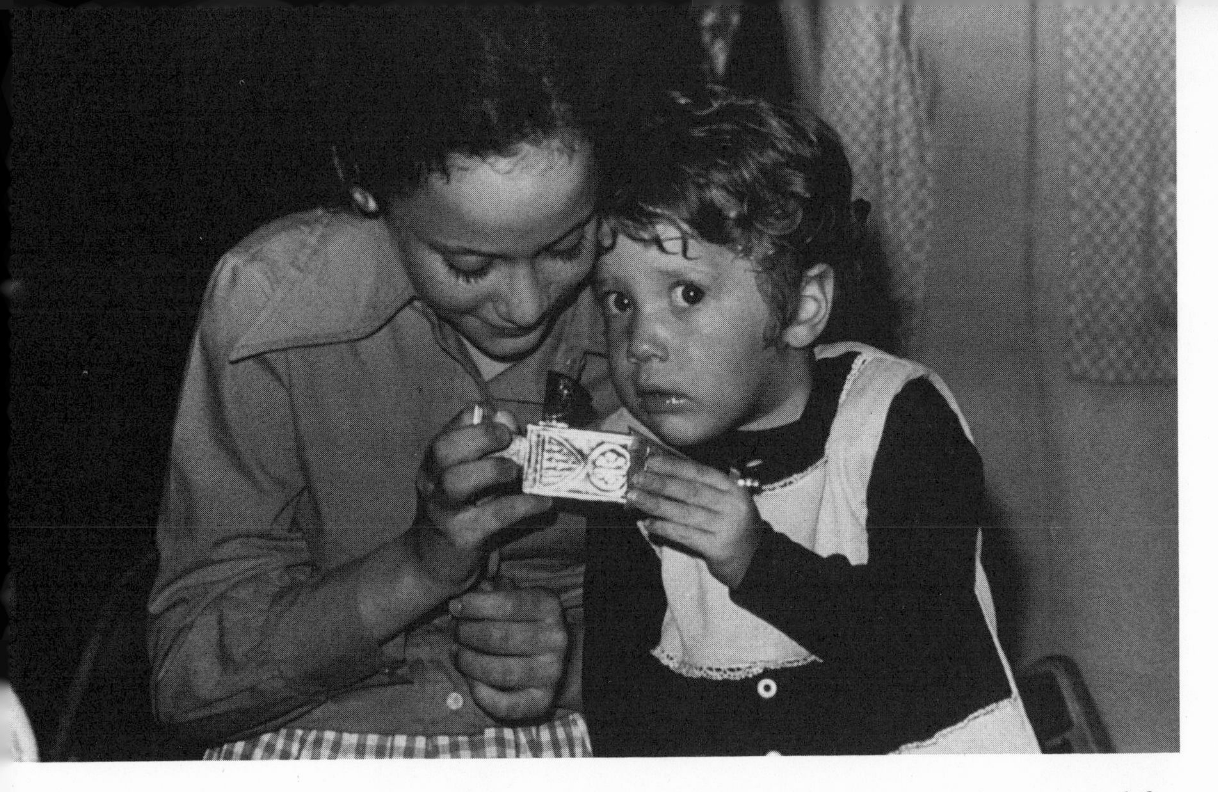

Additional blessings of the Havdalah ritual are recited for fragrant spices (*b'samim*) whose sweet smells are inhaled from the *b'samim* box. The sweet smells are regarded as a delight for the soul, making up for the loss of the Sabbath.

Girls learning to bake *hallah,* the traditional bread used on the Sabbath and other festive occasions.

12

Passover

And ye shall observe the feast of unleavened bread.

—EXODUS 12:17

Passover, probably the best known and most beloved of all the festivals, celebrates the Exodus of the Jews from slavery in Egypt and the years spent wandering in the desert.

Shmura matza (unleavened bread for the festival) is baked in the orthodox community from guarded flour. The flour is guarded from moisture from the time of harvest until it is baked.

Shmura matza is prepared under the supervision of a religious authority to insure its being kosher, and every procedure in the *matza* factory is executed by hand.

Hametz (leavening) is forbidden during Passover, and in order to avoid all contact with it, surfaces on which food is prepared are covered for the duration of the festival, and kitchen utensils and dishes used all year round are locked away or ritually cleansed for Passover use.

Little packets of *hametz* are hidden in the house, searched for, discovered, and destroyed before the start of the holiday.

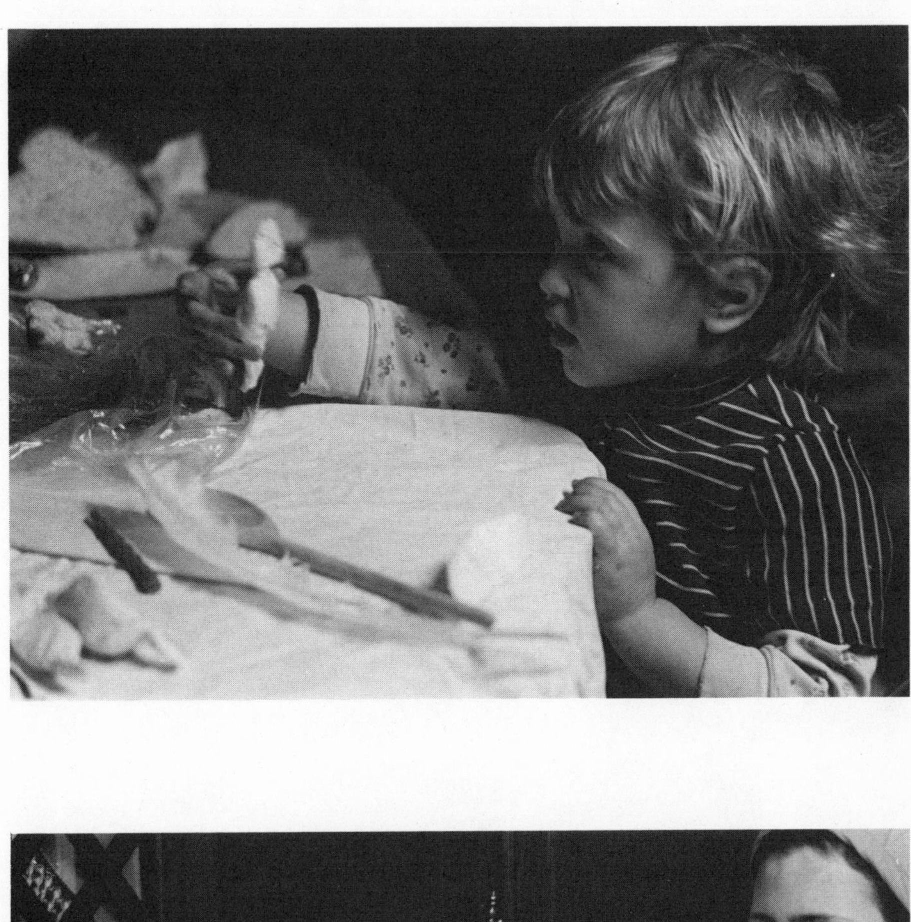

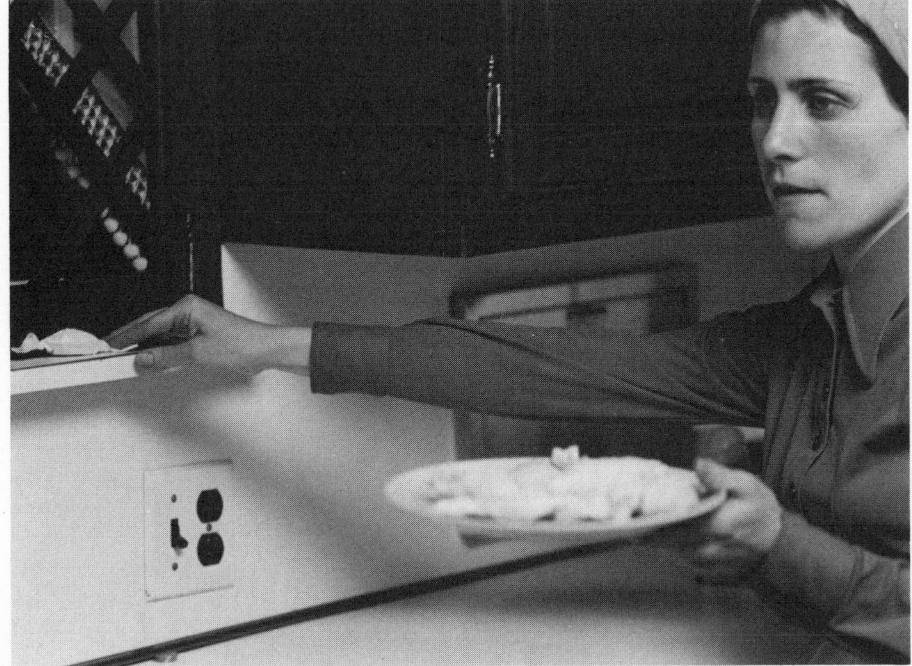

163
163

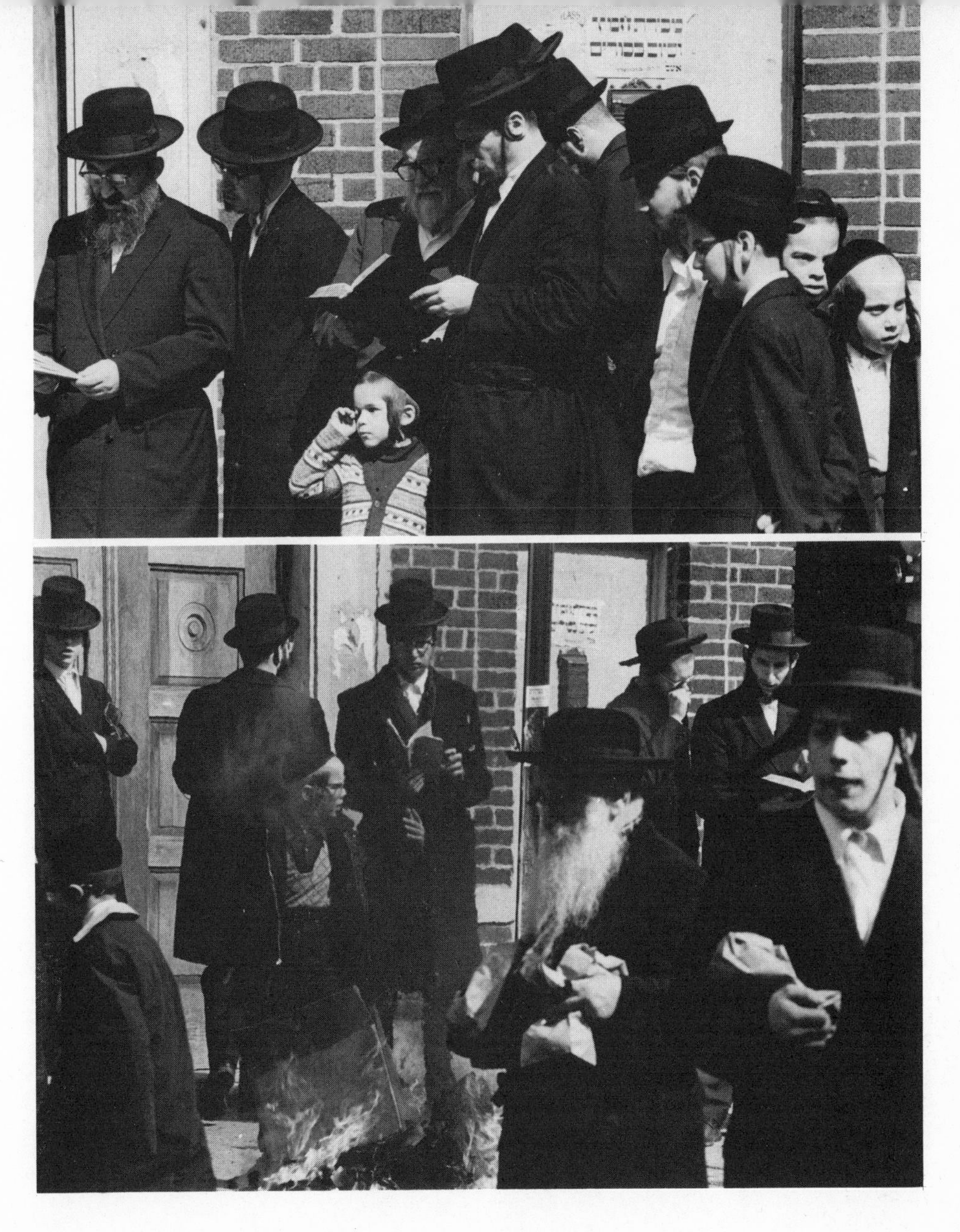

Burning *hametz* before the beginning of Passover.

Preparing *matza* for the Seder table.

The Seder feast at which the Haggadah is read that commemorates the Exodus from Egypt.

The commandment that forbids Jews to eat *hametz* during Passover has given rise to a group of products that allow observant Jews to comply with the rules and enjoy the conveniences and fashion of modern society.

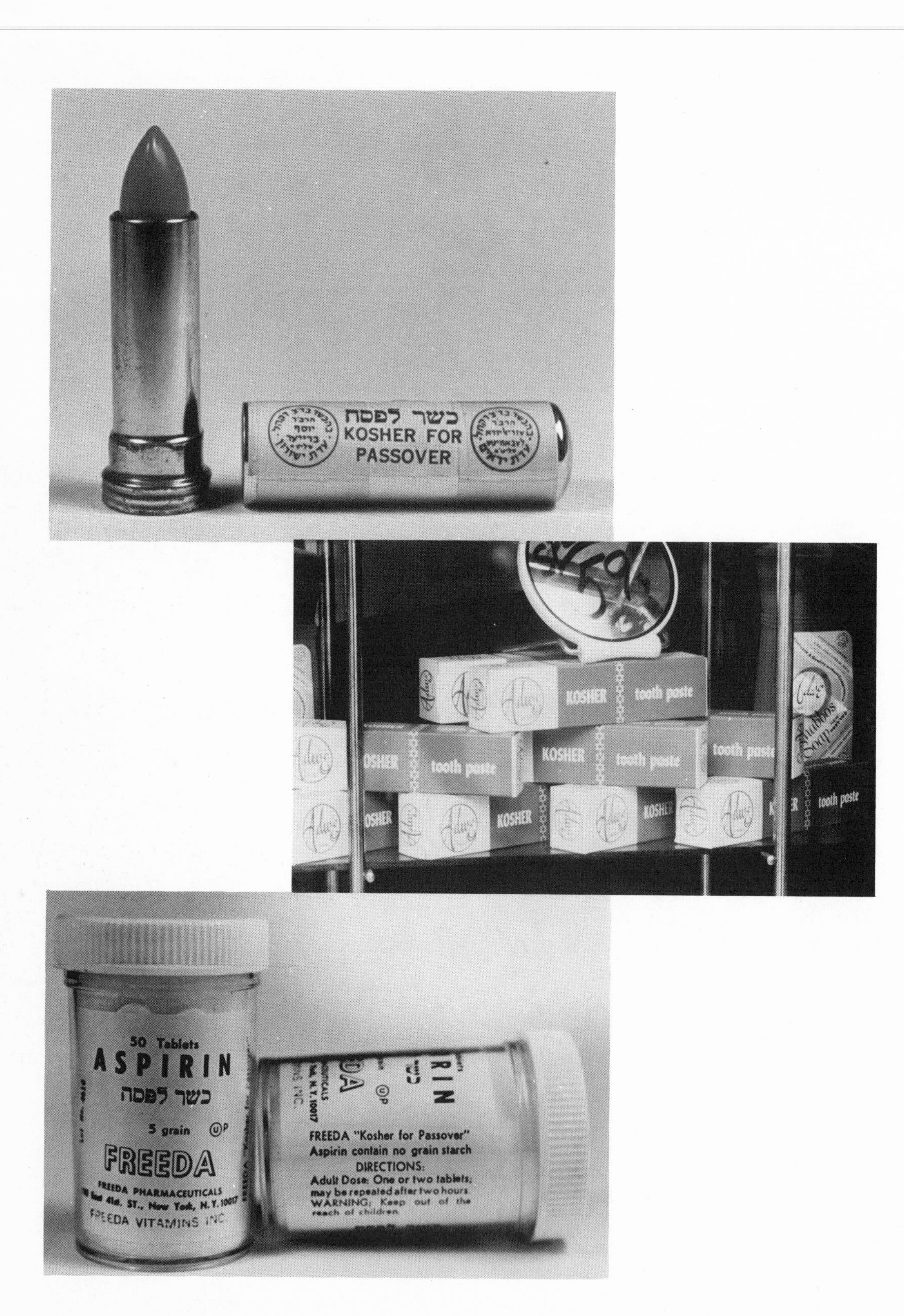

13
Lag B'Omer

In the second century an outbreak of plague among the pupils of Rabbi Akiva ended on Lag B'Omer (the 33rd day of the Omer). Traditionally school children are given a holiday and the day is celebrated with a parade.

לשנה הבאה
PUT ON TEFILLIN
WE'RE FROM BORO PARK
WE'RE FROM BORO PARK

The reviewing stand.

New York City Mayor Abraham Beame in the reviewing stand.

14
Rosh Hashanah and Yom Kippur

In the seventh month, in the first day of the month, shall be a solemn rest unto you, a memorial proclaimed with a blast of horns, a holy convocation.

—LEVITICUS 23:24

Prior to Rosh Hashanah it is the custom to write a *kvittl* (prayer note) to be left at the grave of a *tzaddik* (righteous man).

Rosh Hashanah (New Year) is marked in the synagogue with a blast of the *shofar* (ram's horn).

Howbeit on the tenth day of this seventh month is the day of atonement.

—LEVITICUS 23:27

In preparation for the fast of Yom Kippur (day of atonement), charity money is brought to the synagogue prior to the evening services for distribution to various religious and social welfare institutions.

Rosh Hashanah and Yom Kippur, "The Days of Awe," are a time of penitance and prayer.

15

Sukkot

And ye shall take you on the first day the fruit of goodly trees, branches of palm trees, and boughs of thick trees, and willows of the brook, and ye shall rejoice before the Lord your God seven days.

—LEVITICUS 23:40

Ye shall dwell in booths seven days.

—LEVITICUS 23:42

Every day during the seven-day festival, observant Jews pray with a *lulav* (a bouquet made up of the three required plants) and *etrog* (representing "the fruit of goodly trees").

On the way to the synagogue to celebrate the festival.

NO
STANDING
WILSON

Prior to the festival there is a lively commerce in the sale of *lulav* and *etrogs*.

During the festival observant Jews take all their meals in a *sukkah* (booth). This is a *sukkah* in back of a delicatessen in Brooklyn.

Every year the Lubavitch youth movement sends out *sukkah* mobiles in which Jews are invited to say a blessing with a *lulav* and *etrog*.

The Lubavitcher Rebbe passes out honey cake from his private *sukkah*.

On Hoshana Raba, the seventh day of the holiday, *Sefer Torahs* are brought to the *bima* (reading desk) in the synagogue.

16

Hanukkah

Hanukkah (dedication) commemorates the victory of the Maccabees, and is celebrated in the synagogue and at home by lighting the eight-branched *menorah* (candelabrum).

A *dreidl*, a gambling top, is a Hanukkah tradition.

17

Purim

Therefore do the Jews of the villages, that dwell in the unwalled towns, make the fourteenth day of the month of Adar a day of gladness and feasting, and a good day, and of sending portions one to another.

—ESTHER 9:19

Purim is celebrated in the synagogue by reading the *Megillah,* the scroll containing the story of Mordecai and Esther, telling how the Jews gathered to defend themselves against their enemies in fifth century B.C.E. Persia.

Jewish children dress up in costume and collect "tribute" (money for charity).

The *Megillah* is also read at home.

Whenever the name of Haman, the persecutor of the Jews, is mentioned, children use noisemakers to drown out his name.

Upon completion of the *Megillah,* there is often dancing in the synagogue.

כתר תורה

18
Children

Childhood in the orthodox community, not unlike childhood elsewhere, is filled with swimming and baseball and play—along with the traditional emphasis on prayer and study.

CAMP
EMUNAH

SUN-RAY ROOM

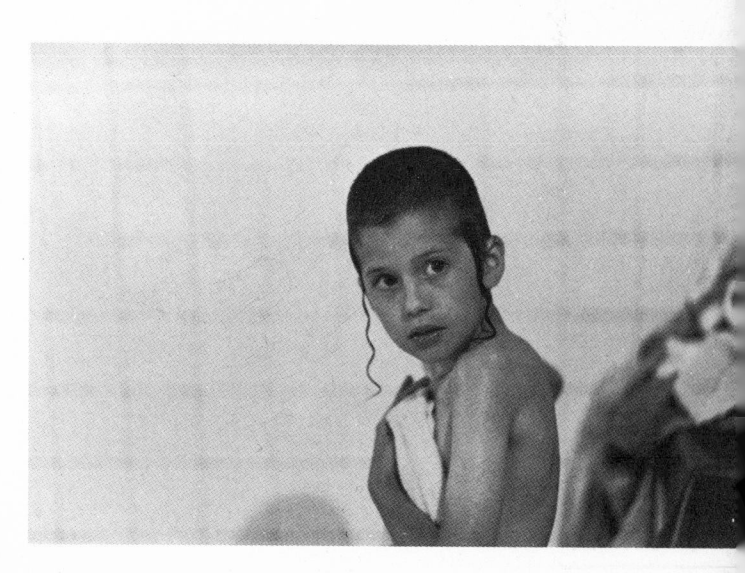

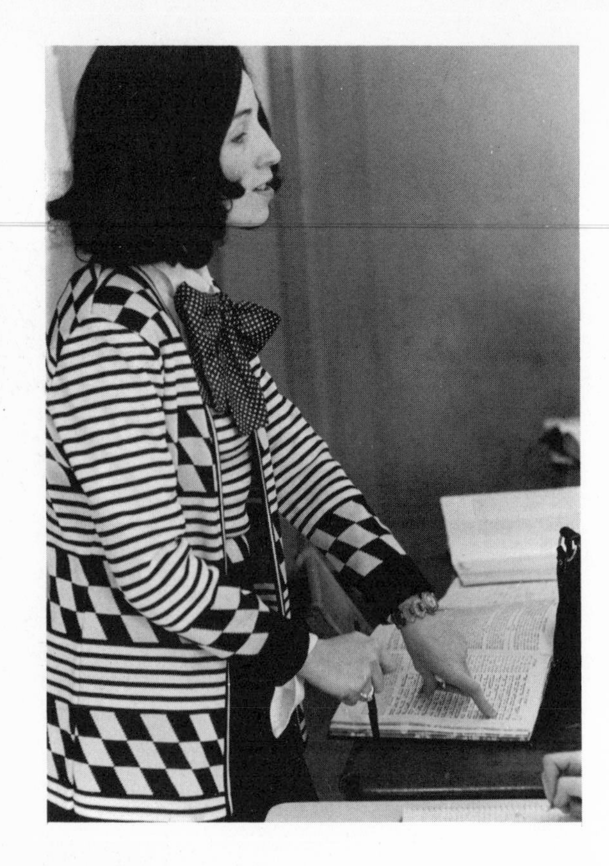

HIGH
BAIS RIVKAH
Bais Rivkah

לכבוד שבת
קודש

19

Daily Life

The daily life of the observant Jew is a continuing affirmation of his encounter with God; Jewish traditions are maintained and, in some instances, interpreted and adapted to fit the conditions of modern urban society.

Manhattan and Brooklyn scenes.

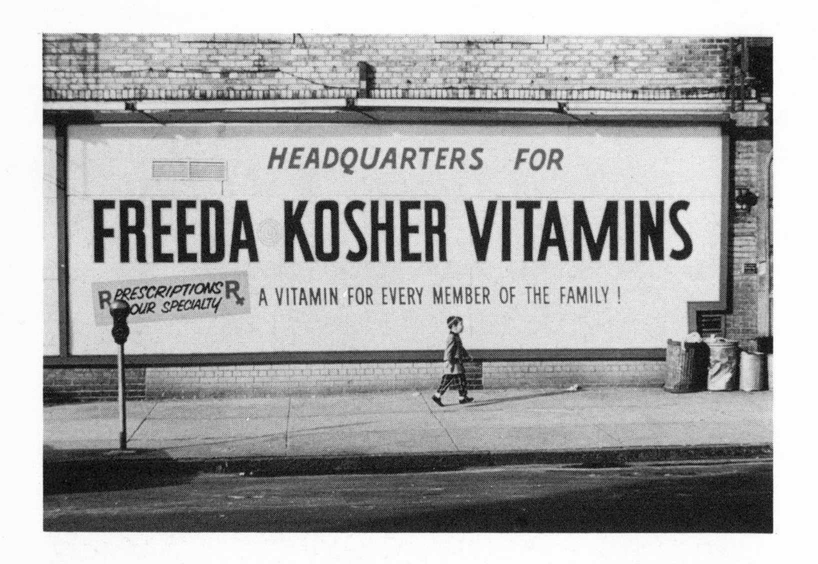

DAIRY
שר
RESTAURA
BEST EMBROIDERY
CO.
Manufacturers of
POROCHESEM, MANTLES
BAR MITZVAH SETS
פרוכתן, מענטאלאך:
טישטיכער, טלית בעגס
חלה און מצה קאווערס
WHOLESALE & RETAIL
רב א. דייטש
סופר
ס'ת'ם
פרי תורה תפלין
מזוזות טליתים
מארץ ישראל
RABBI L. DEUTSCH
43
DISCOUNT HOUS
SONY
SUPERSCOP
TAPE RECO
S. FRIEDMAN

GIMBELS
KOSHER WORLD
KOSHER WORLD
HIRSCH ANTIQUES
Star Barbers
RESTAURANT

TAXI
NO PARKING TAXI STAND
Sam's FAMOUS · כשר ·
KNISHES · PIZZA
Israel's Favourite
FALLAFEL
SHOMER SHABOS
STRICTLY כשר
SICILIAN PIZZA
JUST A REMINDER
502

GOLD
LUNCHEON
COFFEE SHOP

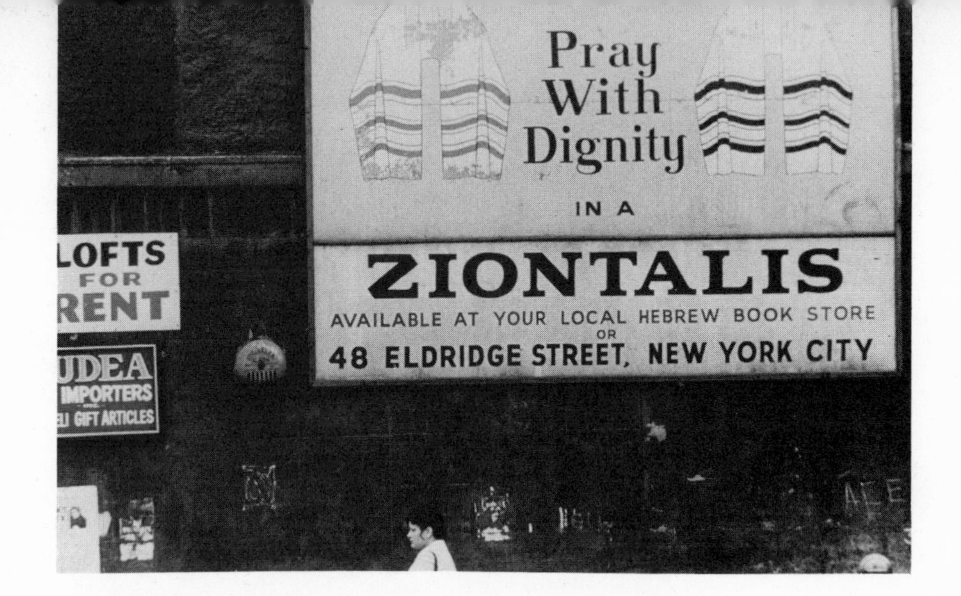
Pray
With
Dignity
IN A
ZIONTALIS
AVAILABLE AT YOUR LOCAL HEBREW BOOK STORE
OR
48 ELDRIDGE STREET, NEW YORK CITY
LOFTS
FOR
RENT
IMPORTERS

Reinman's
SEFORIM
CENTER
מרכז
הספרים
29
Reinman's SEFORIM CENTER
מרכז הספרים
IMPORTERS & PUBLISHERS OF
HEBREW & ENGLISH BOOKS
LEIBEL
BISTRITZKY
KOSHER SPECIALTIES
IMPORTED
DOMESTIC
CHEESE
ISRAELI PRODUCTS
31
podell

Brooklyn scenes: Williamsburg and Crown Heights.

ONE WAY

NO
SNOW
EMERGENCY
STREET

119

The *glatt kosher* butchers.

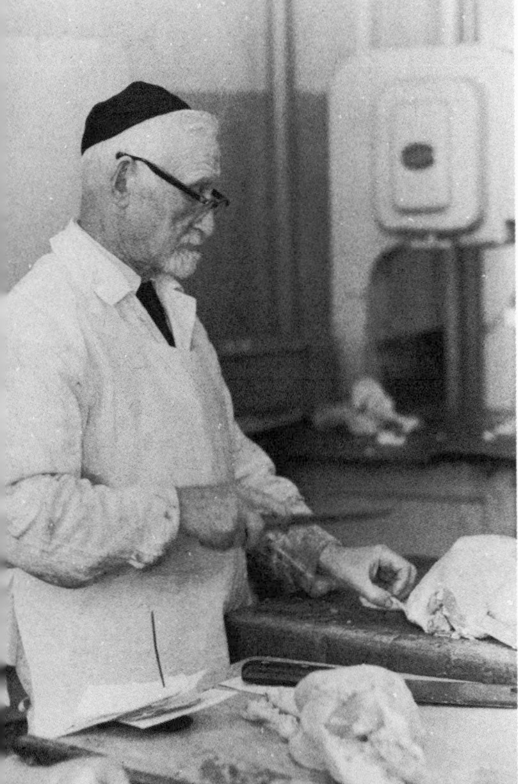

The book sellers.

The painter.

The printer.

The diamond cutters.

Solidarity Day (for Soviet Jewry) at the U.N. Plaza.

20
Brit Milah and *Pidyon Haben*

This is my covenant, which ye shall keep, between you and me and thy seed after thee: every male among you shall be circumcised.

—GENESIS 17:10

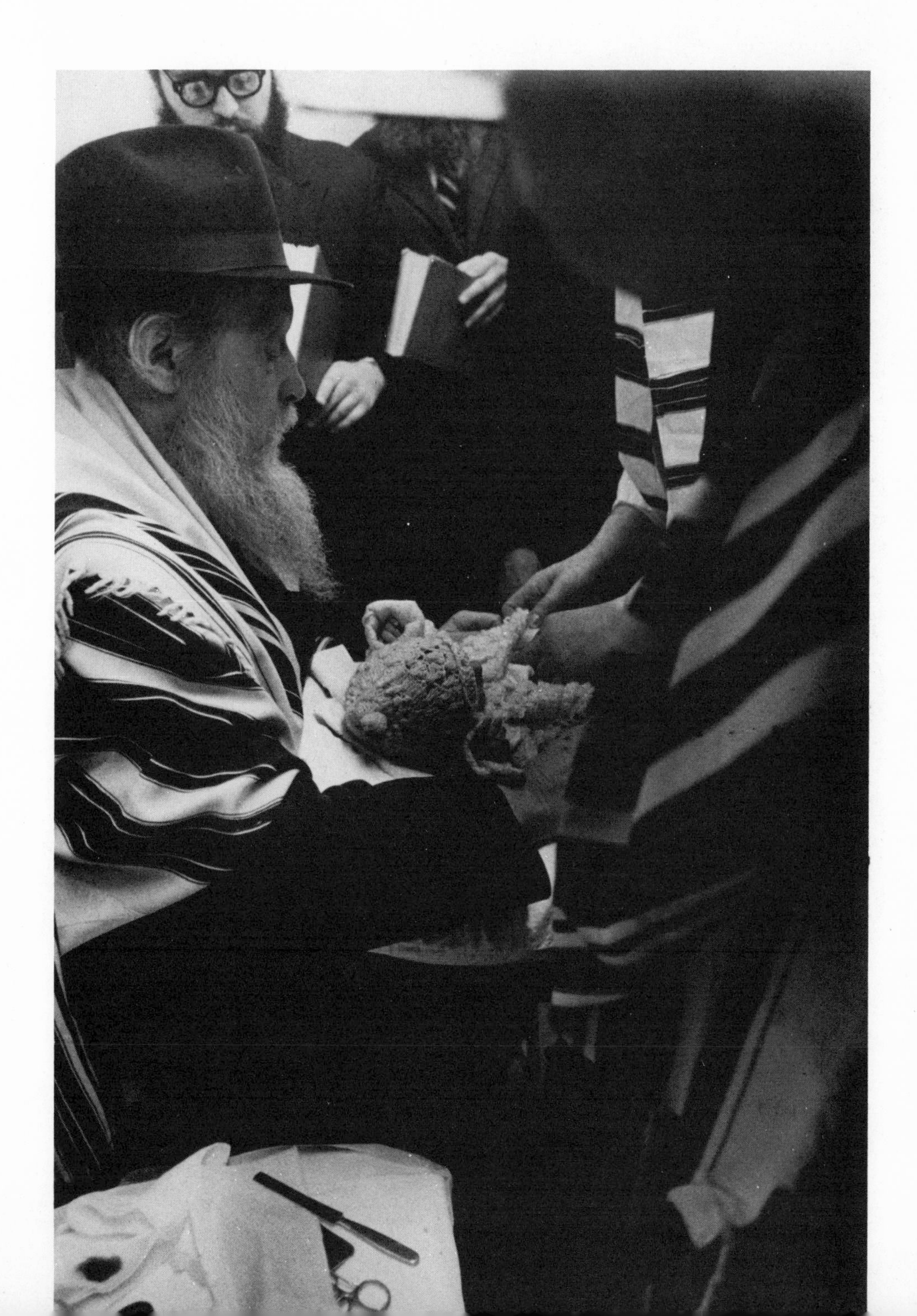

Brit milah (covenant of circumcision).

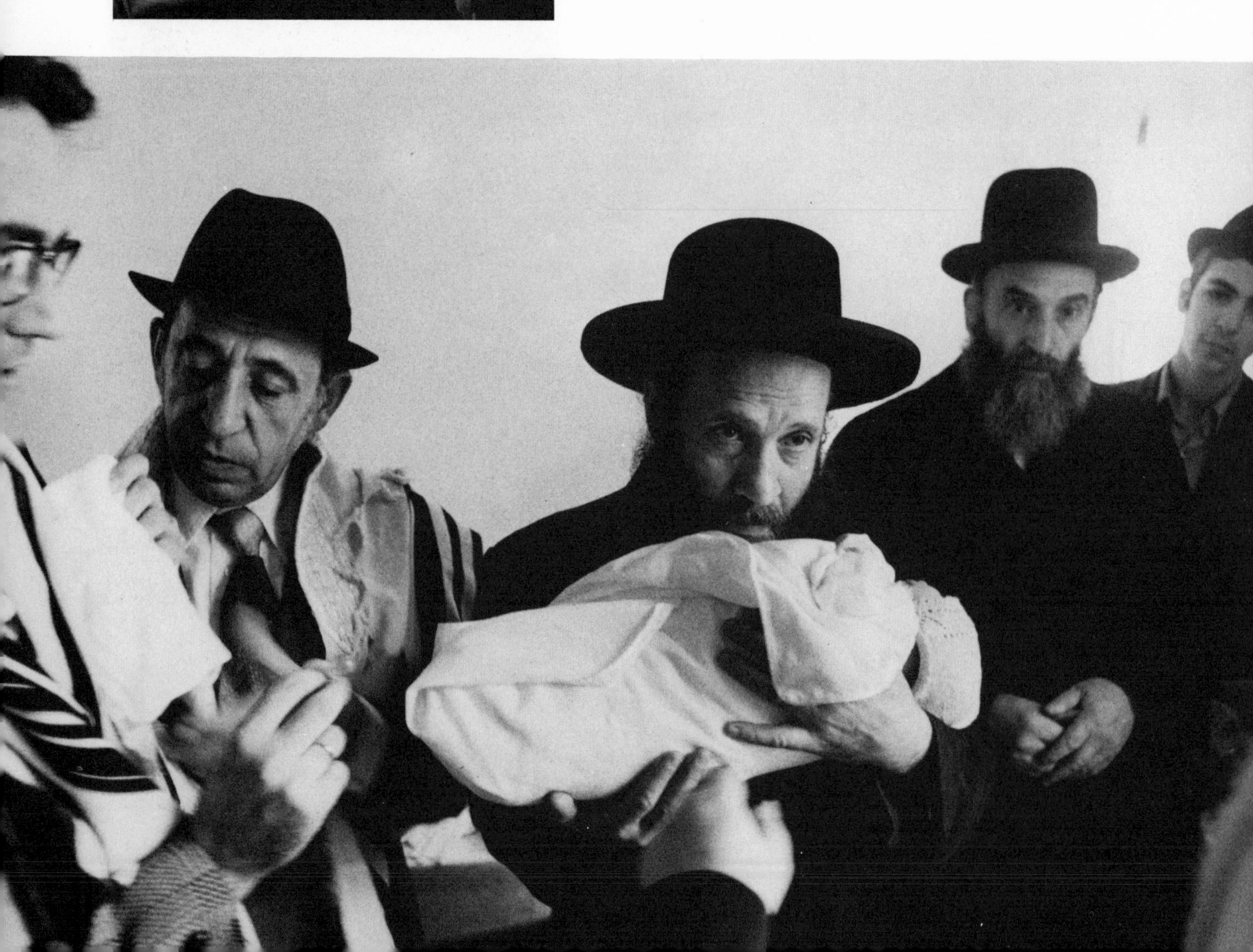

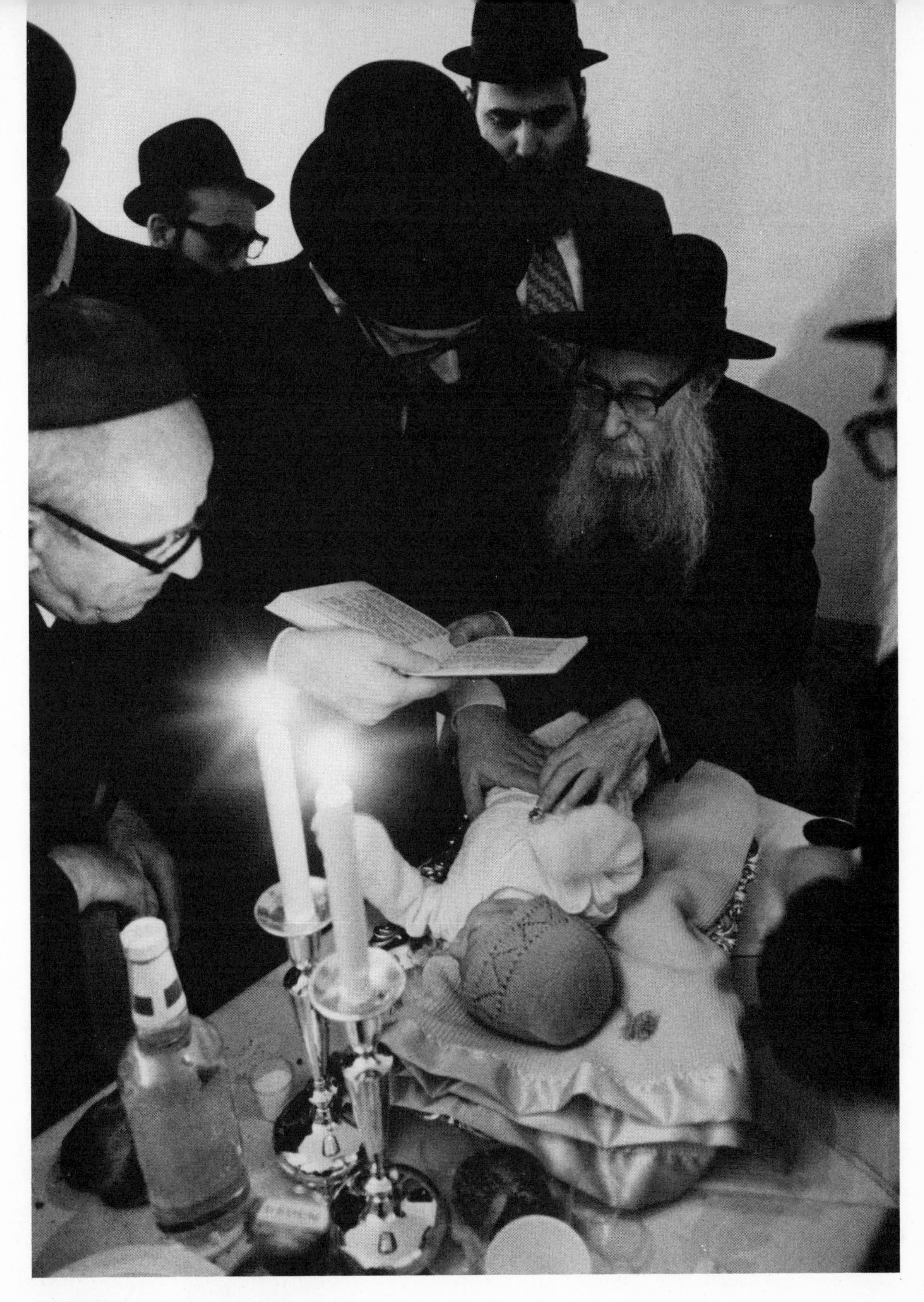

The first born of man shalt thou surely redeem.

—NUMBERS 18:15

The ceremony is called a *pidyon haben,* in which a Jew redeems from a *kohen* (a descendant of the priests) the first born son of a mother.

21
Bar Mitzvah

Bar mitzvah, which means "he who is subject to the commandments," is a religious legal term which marks the thirteenth birthday of a Jewish boy, when he assumes responsibility for the observance of all the precepts and laws.

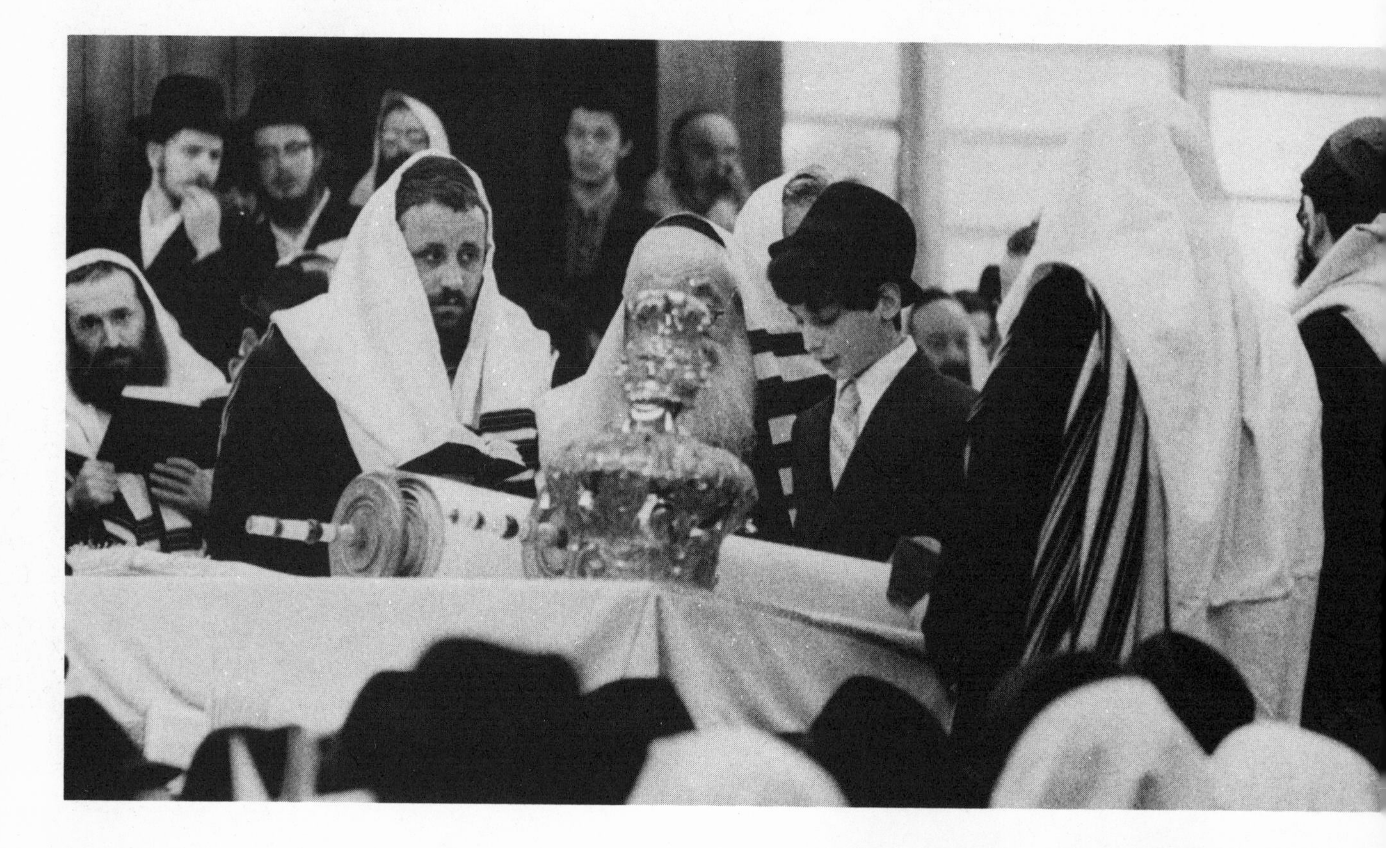

The bar mitzvah reads from the Torah in the synagogue during a regular service to symbolize the attainment of his maturity.

The feast for the bar mitzvah is begun by the blessing for the bread.

In the orthodox community it is customary for the bar mitzvah to deliver (from memory) a learned address on some biblical theme.

Dancing, one of the expressions of joy and ecstasy that mark the occasion.

22
Farbrengen

The *farbrengen* (gathering) is a tradition celebrated by the Lubavitch Hasidic community commemorating holidays and other special occasions.

The Lubavitcher Rebbe,
Manachem Mendel Schneersohn.

Lubavitcher Hasidim gather in the large hall to hear the Rebbe.

Zalman Shazar, then President of Israel, arrives at Crown Heights to see the Rebbe and attend a *farbrengen*.

New York City Mayor Abraham Beame at a *farbrengen* celebrating the Rebbe's birthday.

Jan Peerce and Herman Wouk give birthday greetings to the Rebbe.

People of all ages attend a *farbrengen.*

A *farbrengen* for women.

23

Betrothal – Vort/Tenaim

Be fruitful and multiply.

—GENESIS 1:22

The *vort* (word) is the event that marks a betrothal. Each party pledges their word (there is no written document) in the *kabbalat kinyan*—releasing the handkerchief—a custom based on an ancient Jewish law involving the transfer of property.

In the Lubavitch community the wedding is usually preceded by reading the *tenaim* (the engagement contract).

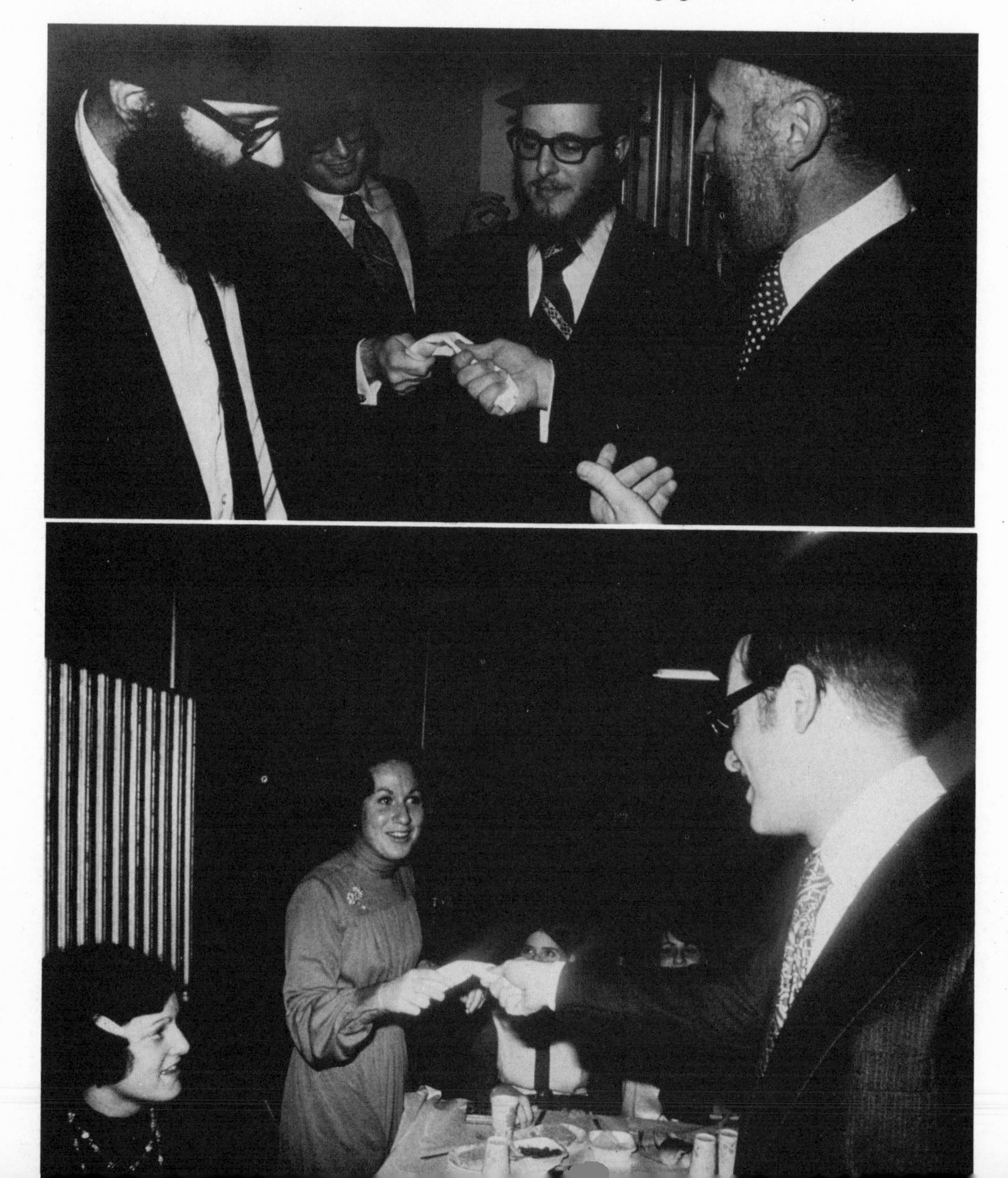

24
Wedding

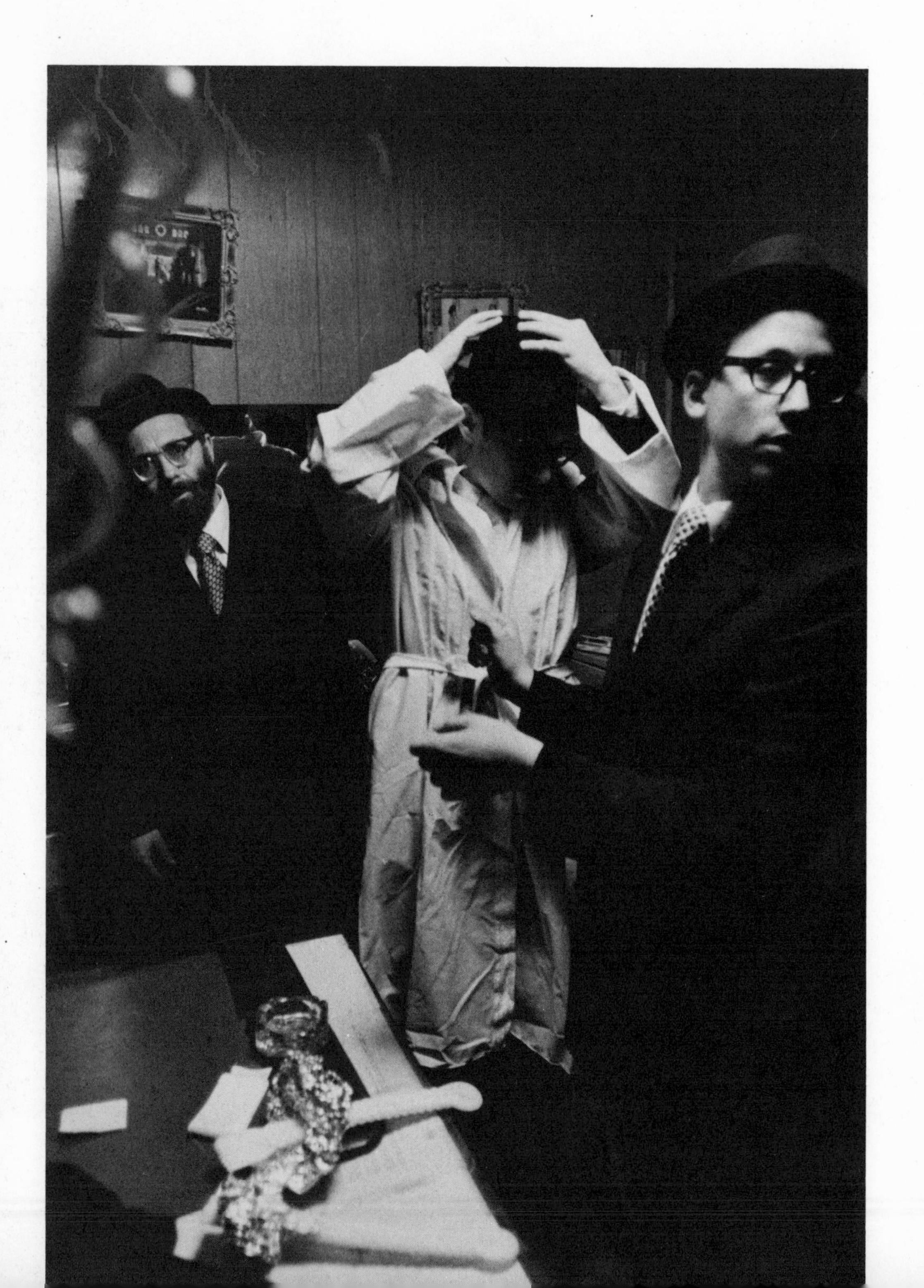

The day of the marriage is considered a day of atonement; this is indicated by donning the *kittl* (a white robe symbolizing purity).

The bride remains veiled until after the ceremony.

A Hasidic bride and groom on their way to the *huppah* (a canopy hung on four poles under which all marriages are performed).

The ceremony is followed by a feast.

Separation of the sexes is maintained by a *mehitzah* (divider, or wall).

Music, dancing, and expressions of joy and happiness are part of the celebration.

Men and women dance separately.

25

Death

For dust thou art, and unto dust shalt thou return.

—GENESIS 3:19

The hearse being followed by mourners and the Lubavitcher Rebbe.

Visiting cemeteries to offer prayers and to petition aid at the graves of the departed is an age-old custom.

Candles burning outside the grave of a *tzaddik* (righteous man).

Kohanim (descendants of priests) are forbidden by law to have contact with the dead. They are protected by their friends forming a ring around them.

The graveside of a *tzaddik* is considered holy ground.